Oxford Progressive English Readers provide a wide range of enjoyable reading at six language levels. Text lengths range from 8,000 words at the Starter level, to about 35,000 words at Level 5. The latest methods of text analysis, using specially designed software, ensure that readability is carefully controlled.

The aim of the series is to present stories to engage the interest of the reader; to intrigue, mystify, amuse, delight and stimulate the imagination.

THE GOLDEN TOUCH AND OTHER STORIES

Edited by David Foulds

OXFORD
UNIVERSITY PRESS

OXFORD
UNIVERSITY PRESS

Oxford University Press is a department of the University of Oxford.
It furthers the University's objective of excellence in research, scholarship,
and education by publishing worldwide in

Oxford New York

Auckland Cape Town Dar es Salaam Hong Kong Karachi
Kuala Lumpur Madrid Melbourne Mexico City Nairobi
New Delhi Shanghai Taipei Toronto

With offices in

Argentina Austria Brazil Chile Czech Republic France Greece
Guatemala Hungary Italy Japan South Korea Poland Portugal
Singapore Switzerland Thailand Turkey Ukraine Vietnam

Oxford is a registered trade mark of Oxford University Press

© Oxford University Press 1992, 2005

First published 1992
Second edition published 2005

This impression (lowest digit)
9 11 13 15 14 12 10 8

All rights reserved. No part of this publication may be reproduced,
stored in a retrieval system, or transmitted, in any form or by any means,
without the prior permission in writing of Oxford University Press,
or as expressly permitted by Law, or under terms agreed with the appropriate
reprographics rights organization. Enquiries concerning reproduction
outside the scope of the above should be sent to the Rights Department,
Oxford University Press, at the address below

You must not circulate this book in any other binding or cover
and you must impose the same condition on any acquirer

Illustrated by Choy Man Yung

Syllabus design and text analysis by David Foulds

ISBN: 978-0-19-597139-2

Printed in Hong Kong
Published by Oxford University Press (China) Ltd
18th Floor, Warwick House East, Taikoo Place, 979 King's Road, Quarry Bay
Hong Kong

CONTENTS

	Introduction	vi
1	The Golden Touch	1
2	The First Spider	9
3	The Donkey's Ears	18
4	Theseus and the Minotaur	26
5	The Wonderful Wings	37
6	Pluto and Persephone	45
7	A Wonderful Musician	53
8	The Golden Chariot of the Sun	59
	Questions and Activities	70

INTRODUCTION

These stories are thousands of years old. They come from ancient Greece. In the days when these stories were first told, most people believed in gods and goddesses. They also believed in heroes and monsters and magic weapons.

In those days, people told stories to explain the world around them. The sun was a fiery chariot and it was pulled by fierce, fast horses. When people died, a dark boatman took them across the river of death to the kingdom of the dead. And the spider was once a clever young woman.

In *The Golden Touch*, King Midas asks a god for a wish. The god gives Midas what he asks for; but it does not make him happy. Instead, he loses the thing he loves most.

Scientists have a special name for spiders. They call them Arachnidae. In *The First Spider*, a girl called Arachne makes the goddess Minerva angry. You will find out how Minerva punishes Arachne.

In *The Donkey's Ears*, King Midas appears again. But still he has not learnt his lesson. The story shows that sometimes even a king could be foolish. It also shows that some people find it very difficult to keep a secret.

Many old buildings have lots of corridors and it is very easy to get lost in them. There is a labyrinth under the palace of King Minos. A clever engineer called Daedalus has built it for the King. It is the home of Minos's monster, the Minotaur. In *Theseus and the Minotaur* we meet a brave young man, and the clever young woman who helps him find his way through the labyrinth.

In *The Wonderful Wings* we actually meet the engineer, Daedalus. He does not like people less clever than himself. One day he makes King Minos angry, and the King decides to punish his rude servant. Minos locks Daedalus and his young son Icarus in prison at the top of a high tower. But Daedalus finds a way to escape.

Why do we have winter? Why can't it be summer all year round? Of course, we all know the seasons are caused by the Earth's journey round the sun. But *Pluto and Persephone* makes a more interesting story!

Music is a wonderful thing. It can make strong, hard people cry. It can make lazy people dance. The musician Orpheus goes to the kingdom of the dead to look for his dead wife. His music makes a terrible three-headed guard dog as gentle as a kitten. It even touches the heart of the dark god Pluto. Can Orpheus save his wife?

In *The Golden Chariot of the Sun*, a boy called Phaeton believes his father is dead. Then one day his mother tells him a secret. His father is not dead. He is the sun-god Apollo! And so Phaeton sets out to find his father.

Read on to find out more.

1
THE GOLDEN TOUCH

Midas

Some people are very lucky. When we talk about these people, we say 'He has the Midas touch,' or 'Everything she touches turns to gold.' By that we mean everything is done well. We do not mean that everything really turns to gold.

But long ago, that did happen to one person. He prayed for the golden touch. The gods granted his wish. From that time on, everything he touched really did turn into gold, but it did not make him happy.

That person was a king called Midas. He had everything — a beautiful palace with wonderful flower gardens, plenty of money and a loving family. He had whole rooms full of gold, but he always wanted more. Gold was the most important thing in his life. When he prayed to the gods, he did not pray to be happy. He did not pray to be a good king. He just hoped, wished and prayed for more gold. Every day he thought about it and at night he dreamt about it.

A visitor

In those days one of the gods, called Dionysus, would often come down from heaven and spend some time on the Earth. Dionysus was the god of wine. He liked to drink wine all the time. His best friend was Silenus. Silenus was a satyr. From his waist up to his head he looked like a man but under his long hair were large, hairy ears like a goat's ears. From his waist down he was a goat. He had hairy legs and a tail and little hoofs at the end of each leg. He was Dionysus's greatest friend, and the two of them would often drink wine together.

One morning King Midas went for a walk in his flower garden. There he found Silenus asleep. He was lying under a small tree. There were several empty wine bottles beside him and there was a happy smile on his foolish face.

Midas shouted to his servants. They at once took hold of Silenus and made him a prisoner. They put him in a small room, and locked the door. Silenus did not mind much. He just lay down in his new bed and fell asleep again. Midas ordered his men to be kind to him. He was a greedy king, but he was not cruel.

Dionysus looked everywhere for his friend. At last he found out where Silenus was, and came to see Midas. He begged the King to let his friend go.

'He did not mean to come into your garden,' said Dionysus. 'Please let me take him home. If you do, I will grant you a wish.'

'*Any* wish?' said Midas. He thought about gold, whole palaces made of gold, ships full of gold. What should he wish for? Suddenly he had an idea. 'I wish,' he said aloud, 'that everything I touch will turn to gold.'

The wish is granted

Dionysus looked hard at the greedy king. 'Are you quite sure?' he asked. 'You want everything you touch to turn to gold?'

'That's right,' said Midas. 'Take your friend. He is awake now. His head hurts him very much because he drank too much wine. Now grant me my wish! Let everything I touch turn to gold.'

'Your wish is granted already,' said the god. He gave a small, secret smile. 'And if you change your mind, just call for me.'

'I shall not change my mind!' said Midas. 'Thank you, Dionysus, for granting my wish.'

As soon as Dionysus and Silenus had gone, Midas tested his new skill. He touched a large table. It became cold, hard metal. It shone like the sun.

'Gold!' cried Midas. 'It works!' Laughing like a naughty little boy, he touched all the walls of the room. They turned to gold, too. 'I am rich!' shouted the King. 'I'm the richest man in all the world!' He touched the curtains at the windows. At once they hung in stiff gold folds.

Midas sang and shouted. A small insect flew in through the window. It landed on Midas's nose. At once it fell down dead on the floor. Midas picked it up and looked at it carefully. The insect was all gold, head, body, wings and legs. It looked like a very lovely piece of jewellery.

'Now I do not need to buy gold jewellery for my wife. I can make it myself! I will make gold presents for my little daughter, too,' Midas said.

Midas spent hours practising. He changed everything in the room into gold. Then he went out into his flower garden. He found Silenus's empty bottles. He changed those into gold. Then he started on the garden itself. Soon it was full of stiff, dead, gold flowers, trees and grass. He could not touch the birds. They were too quick for him. They flew among the golden trees. They did not know why the leaves were such a funny yellow colour.

Midas picked a big bunch of gold flowers. He took them into the palace and put them in a vase. The vase changed to gold as soon as he touched it.

'I really am the richest man in the whole world,' said Midas to himself. 'I have the golden touch. Thank you, great Dionysus, for granting my wish.'

The gold statue

Just then there was a knock at the door. 'Come in!' called the King. The door opened and his little daughter entered. She was a sweet, pretty child and the King loved her very much.

'How strange everything looks, Father,' the child said. She looked in surprise at the gold room. She picked up the little gold insect from the table.

'What a pretty little thing,' she said. 'It is just like a real insect.'

'It is better than a real insect, dear,' said her father. 'It is made of gold.'

'I like your flowers, Father,' the girl said. She touched the gold flowers in their gold vase. 'They look just like real ones.' She held a stiff gold flower near her nose. 'What a pity they have no smell.'

King Midas watched her. To him she seemed the loveliest thing in his whole kingdom. Without thinking, he reached out and touched her hand.

At once her body became cold and stiff. King Midas was not holding his daughter. He was holding a beautiful gold statue.

'What have I done?' he cried. He shouted for his servants. They could not understand what had happened, and they were unhappy. The King was too hurt and sad to explain. The servants carried the beautiful gold statue upstairs. They laid it on the bed. Midas's queen hurried forward to him.

He stepped back with a cry. 'Don't touch me!' he screamed. 'Can't you see? Everything I touch turns to gold. Look what happened to our child! Keep away!' He ran upstairs and lay down on his bed.

Hunger and thirst

He could not sleep that night. As soon as he laid his head on the pillow it became hard and cold.

His stiff gold bed was not warm enough. He was lonely without his wife. He was afraid to lie next to her, of course. He did not want to find another gold statue beside him in the morning.

When he got up he was very hungry and thirsty. He could not eat or drink, however. Every bite of food turned to gold in his mouth. He tried to drink some water. Every drop turned to gold. He had to spit it out.

'I shall die of hunger and thirst!' he said. Now he could see the danger he was in. He was the richest man in the world, but he was going to die like a beggar. 'What can I do?' he cried.

The Queen was a gentle, wise woman. 'Ask Dionysus to help you,' she said. 'He granted your wish, so he must be able to take it away again.'

Midas knew that she was right. He remembered that Dionysus had said, 'If you change your mind, just call for me.'

He went out into the flower garden and began to pray. At once Dionysus appeared before him. The god was smiling.

'Well,' said Dionysus, looking around, 'I see you have been busy. Has your golden touch made you happy?'

Midas fell on his knees. 'It has made me very sad,' he said. He told the story of his little daughter. 'I miss her terribly,' he said. 'And now I understand that I am going to die of hunger and thirst, too. Please, please take back the golden touch. I don't want it any more. I want to hold my little daughter in my arms again. I want to kiss my dear wife. I want to eat and drink again. Please, Dionysus, forgive me!'

Midas's wish is granted

'Very well,' said Dionysus. 'I will grant your wish once more. Go to the river and bathe in the water. Then everything will be all right again.'

King Midas ran down to the river and threw himself in. He was surprised. The river water did not turn into gold. When he came out again he touched the grass of the river bank. It remained green and soft. He hurried back to his palace. His little daughter ran to greet him. He held her in his arms.

'Oh, Father,' she said, 'I've had such a strange dream! I dreamt I was a statue. Wasn't that silly?'

Midas looked round his palace. The golden walls, the golden floor, the golden tables and chairs were no longer there. A small insect sat on a curtain. It was cleaning its wings. 'Is it the same insect?' Midas asked himself. 'I shall never know.' He looked out of the window at his gardens. The flowers danced in the sun. The wind blew the lovely green leaves of the trees this way and that. The birds were singing happily.

Servants brought dishes of food and jugs of wine, and Midas ate and drank. To him the simple meal seemed like a feast. He held his queen's hand while his little daughter sat on his knee. 'I will never be greedy again,' he said to himself.

This is only a story, but there is something strange about the river in Midas's kingdom. Its sand has gold in it. If you put the sand in some water and move it round and round, small pieces of gold dust will appear.

2
THE FIRST SPIDER

Spiders

Many people hate spiders. They think spiders are ugly. Some people are even afraid of them. Housewives do not like the webs that spiders make to catch flies and other insects. The webs make their nice clean homes look dirty. But if you go into a garden and see the spiders' webs there, you may think differently. If you look closely you will see that the webs are made very cleverly, and that they are quite beautiful. Look at the threads they are made of. You will see that they are very thin, but they are also stronger than any threads that people can make.

There are millions of different spiders. In science, they have a special name. They are called Arachnidae. This story tells us why spiders have been given this name.

Minerva and Arachne

Long ago, there was a goddess called Minerva. She was the goddess of knowledge and art. Her father was Jupiter. He was the king of all the gods. Minerva had no mother. One story says that she just jumped straight out of the head of her father, Jupiter, holding a sword in her hand. She was a fierce goddess as well as a clever one, and if anyone made her angry she could be very cruel.

In those days there was a poor farmer who lived in a little house with his wife and daughter. The girl's name was Arachne. When she was still quite small she began to show that she was very clever with thread and cloth. Soon she became famous. She was able to sell her work for high prices and her skill made the whole family quite rich.

By the time Arachne was grown up, people were travelling long distances to see her work. She could take wool from the coats of sheep and make it into the softest, strongest, thinnest thread in the world.

She would take many different threads and weave them under and over one another in order to make beautiful cloth. Then she would cover the cloth with pictures using different coloured threads. Her busy needle shot in and out of the cloth like flashes of lightning. Flowers and fruit, birds and clouds appeared there like magic.

'How wonderful!' everyone cried. 'What skill! What art!'

Rich and important people praised Arachne. They gave her large amounts of money for her pictures.

At first she did not like it when they praised her. In her heart she was still just a girl from a poor, simple family. She hid her hot, red face in her hands and looked down at her feet.

Later, however, Arachne became quite used to praise and money. She bought her parents a nice house and she began to feel very pleased with herself.

As good as Minerva!

'I must be special after all,' Arachne said to herself. She became quite proud, and she often boasted about how clever she was to all her visitors.

One day a rich merchant arrived. He had travelled hundreds of miles to meet her. He said he would give her a very high price for a special piece of work. He wanted her to make a picture for his wife. Arachne made the thread. She used leaves and fruit to colour it. She wove a wonderful piece of cloth that was coloured green and blue, brown and gold. She added pictures of flowers and birds and insects. They were so real and lifelike, the merchant could not stop himself from reaching out and touching them.

'I cannot believe this!' he cried. He held the cloth carefully, and touched the beautiful flowers. 'I have never seen anything like it. You make thread and weave it into cloth like a goddess. Only Minerva herself could do better.'

'Who says she could do better?' said Arachne. 'This is my *best* work, sir. No one, no one can make thread or weave it better than I can. I hear that the goddess Minerva sometimes makes cloth in her free time, but have never seen anything that she has done. Perhaps her work is better than mine. I am ready to believe it, but she will have to show me first!'

The goddess heard Arachne's proud words. She was hurt and angry.

'Who does this human think she is?' Minerva said to herself. 'I must pay her a visit and talk to her. Perhaps she boasted a little without thinking what she was saying. If she is sorry, I will excuse her.'

The goddess took off her beautiful dress of purple and gold. She put on a torn old brown coat. She covered her beautiful hair with a black cloth. She took a strong stick, and when she began to walk she leant on it heavily. She used magic to change herself into an old woman with white hair and black, broken teeth. She looked in her mirror. 'That is very good,' she said. 'No one will ever know me like this.'

Arachne receives a visitor

There was a knock at the door of Arachne's house. 'Come in!' she called. She was quite used to visitors. Already a circle of interested people stood around her. They had come to watch Arachne doing her work.

'Sit down,' said Arachne to the old woman. 'I am spinning wool to make thread at the moment.' She had some sheep's wool at her feet. Her busy fingers were spinning the wool into beautiful strong thread. Her hands moved so fast that Minerva could hardly see them.

'When I finish spinning this wool,' said Arachne after a few moments, 'I shall start weaving a new piece of cloth to make a picture. Watch carefully. You do not often see a real artist at work. They say the goddess Minerva herself is jealous of my skill.'

She started her new picture. Trees and hills appeared like magic before the eyes of the people. As she worked, Arachne talked to everyone about how clever she was, and how no one could make pictures as well as she could. Minerva grew more and more angry.

A proud and foolish girl

Minerva stepped forward and laid a gentle hand on the girl's arm.

'Dear child,' she said, 'it is dangerous to boast too loudly about your skill. The gods may hear.'

'I want them to hear!' cried the proud, foolish girl. 'I want them to see for themselves! And if they are jealous, that can only mean they are afraid I am better than they are!'

'Listen to an old woman, dear. I have lived a long time, and I have met many clever, proud young people. Their lives did not always end happily. You spin and weave wonderfully well, but you are only human. Do not compare yourself with the gods. Ask Minerva's pardon for your foolish boasting. I promise you that she will forgive you.'

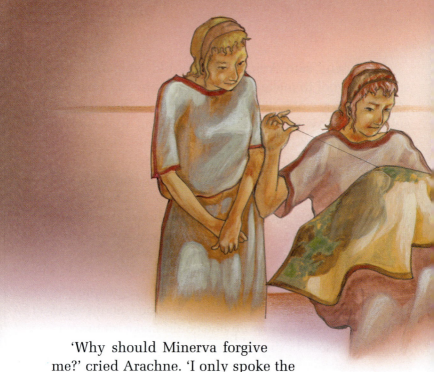

'Why should Minerva forgive me?' cried Arachne. 'I only spoke the truth. You do not understand. You are just a poor old woman, and your mind is as weak as your poor tired old body. I tell you, Minerva should come here and try her skill. I will show everyone that I spoke the truth. I think she must be afraid of the test. Why hasn't she come before?'

Then Minerva dropped her stick and stood up very straight. She tore the black cloth off her hair and she said a magic word. Arachne and the people around her saw the tall goddess standing there. She looked very strong and very beautiful. The other people at once fell on their knees and prayed to Minerva. Arachne was the only one who did not move. She held her head up high and showed no sign of fear.

'So you have come after all!' she said. 'Let us start the test at once, and see which of us is better at spinning and weaving and making beautiful pictures.'

The test

Without another word the goddess and the girl began to work. The people in the room watched. No one spoke; they were almost afraid to breathe.

In the centre of Minerva's piece of cloth a picture began to appear. It was a picture about foolish humans who would not obey the gods. It showed what bad things happened to these people. The goddess hoped that Arachne would look at the picture, and learn a lesson, but Arachne was not frightened at all.

Arachne worked and worked. Her cheeks were pink and she breathed quite fast. Her fingers flew backwards and forwards over the cloth. Soon a picture began to appear. It was so beautiful that it filled the people with joy. You could see hills covered with trees, a bright blue sky with white clouds, and the beautiful dark blue sea. You could almost hear the waves on the seashore. You could almost feel the wind in the trees. You could almost reach out and touch the flowers.

But when the people saw the subject of Arachne's picture, they were afraid. Arachne was telling a story, too. Her story showed that even the gods can sometimes make mistakes.

Minerva is angry

At last both pictures were finished. Now the gods never told lies, and Minerva had to tell the truth about Arachne's work. She had to admit that the girl had won. Arachne's skill was greater than her own.

'You win,' Minerva said. She was angry. She did not like to say that Arachne was better than she was, and she wanted to punish Arachne for that. Arachne saw the angry look on the goddess's face. Suddenly she understood how foolish she had been. She also knew that she was in terrible danger. She wanted to beg Minerva's pardon.

'Forgive me,' she said. But it was too late.

With a scream of anger and hate Minerva picked up Arachne's beautiful cloth. She tore it into small pieces. She threw the pieces at the people. Then she picked up her stick and hit Arachne three times on the head.

Arachne was too proud. She could not live after this terrible moment. She picked up a long rope that was lying near her chair. She tried to hang herself and end her unhappy life.

Minerva held her back. 'No, I won't let you die, you wicked girl! But from this moment, you shall always hang from a thread. You shall spin and weave all your life. And because you are so proud I shall punish you for ever and ever.'

In a moment all Arachne's pretty hair fell off her head. Her face became very small, with great, shining black eyes. Her body became small and black. Her beautiful busy fingers changed into long hairy legs. She was a spider, hanging on a thin thread from a corner of the ceiling.

The people watched as the busy little animal began to weave a web across the corner of the room. The thread was very thin and strong. The web was very beautiful. The first spider was getting ready to catch flies for her supper.

Ever since then, spiders have spun their silk threads and woven their beautiful webs, and the name Arachnidae makes us think about the foolish girl and the jealous goddess.

3
THE DONKEY'S EARS

Apollo and Pan

'A secret is too little for one, enough for two, too much for three.' There is a lot of truth in that saying.

Apollo was the god of music. Nearly everyone agreed that Apollo's music was the most beautiful of all. Only one foolish person did not think so. Here is the story of that person, and how he was punished by Apollo.

Another of the gods liked music too. His name was Pan. He was the god of the woods and rivers, and of the wild animals. Pan looked like a very beautiful human boy, until you saw his ears and legs. He had hairy ears like a goat's. He had goat's legs too. Instead of feet, he stood on two little hoofs.

Pan went out one day and found some reeds growing at the side of a river. They were like tall, strong grass. He picked some of the reeds to make pipes, and he played music on them.

The satyrs and nymphs came to listen. Satyrs looked like men from the waist up but from their waist down they looked like goats. Nymphs were goddesses. They and the satyrs did not live in heaven. They lived on Earth near the woods, hills and streams. They liked Pan's wild, sweet music very much.

Midas hears the music

The music reached human ears too. King Midas was in his flower garden one morning when he heard the sound of Pan's reed pipes. The sweet music pleased him very much. He left his garden and joined the nymphs and satyrs on the river bank. When Pan stopped playing, Midas clapped loudly and shouted for more.

After that the King often listened to Pan's music. He praised it loudly. 'I think it is the best music of all,' the King said. 'Even better than Apollo's.'

This pleased the nymphs and satyrs. Pan was their leader; they did not often see Apollo or hear his music. 'Oh yes,' they all agreed, 'much better than Apollo's.'

Pan enjoyed all the praise and clapping. He became very proud. 'I am greater than Apollo,' he said, 'but we must show everyone that it is true, my friends. We must have a contest!'

When Apollo heard, he did not know whether to laugh or cry. 'Is this a joke?' he said to himself. 'Pan has always enjoyed a little fun. He can't be serious now, can he? Well, I don't mind joining in his little game.'

The contest

The nymphs and satyrs chose the place for the contest. It was the smooth, green side of a hill quite near Midas's palace. They asked the god of the hill to judge the contest. He was a dear old god with long white hair and a sweet, kind face. They asked Midas to sit beside the judge. Midas was very proud and felt most important. Many nymphs and satyrs came and sat on the soft, green grass. They were all eager to begin the contest.

The god Apollo stood in front of the judge. He held his shining gold lyre in his hand. Pan stood beside him on his little hoofs. He held his reed pipes. He saw Midas and smiled and waved to him. At a sign from the judge the contest began.

Pan played first. He lifted his reed pipes to his lips and blew. His music seemed to belong to the woods and rivers. The audience could almost hear the sound of the streams and the wind in the trees. It was wild, sweet, lonely music. It was very beautiful, but it made the audience feel unhappy. It made them want to go home to their forests and hills.

Midas clapped and cheered loudly, but the nymphs and satyrs were strangely silent.

Now it was Apollo's turn to play. He took up his golden lyre, and played and sang for a long time. The nymphs and satyrs sat as still as statues.

Apollo's music was not like Pan's. The sound seemed to reach out and touch everyone's heart. The music was so lovely that there were tears of joy in the nymphs' eyes. The satyrs were very quiet as they listened carefully to the words of Apollo's songs. Midas was the only one who did not look interested.

The winner

At last Apollo finished his song. Everyone stood up. They shouted with joy and clapped until their hands ached. They cheered loudly. All except Midas. He gave a few polite little claps, then he turned to the judge of the contest.

'Very nice,' he said, 'but I still like Pan's music best.'

No one else agreed with the King. The judge said that Apollo was the winner, and the nymphs and satyrs all went to Apollo and stood round him. Pan stood alone under a tree. He looked quite hurt and angry.

'I still like Pan's music best,' said Midas loudly. He turned to go back to his palace.

Apollo heard the King's words. 'Do you?' he said softly. He looked hard at Midas.

'Yes, I do,' said Midas. 'Now excuse me; I must go.'

'There must be something wrong with your ears,' said Apollo. He reached out and touched the King's head. 'Goodbye, dear King Midas,' he said. 'Remember me.'

The donkey's ears

Next morning Midas woke up. He got out of bed, washed, and then began to comb his hair. There was something big and soft on the left side of his head. He felt it. It was covered with hair. He felt the right side of his head. There was something there too. Something big and soft and covered with hair. He ran to the mirror. He could not believe what he saw. Instead of his own small, pink ears he had the large, brown, hairy ears of a donkey.

'Someone has played a joke on me,' he said to himself. 'A good joke too! I'll just pull these silly ears off, then I'll have a laugh.' He pulled at the soft brown ears but cried out in pain. The ears were part of him; it was not a joke!

Suddenly Midas remembered that Apollo had touched his head the day before. He remembered the god's words: 'There must be something wrong with your ears.'

So that was how Apollo had decided to punish him! What could he do?

'I mustn't let anyone know,' said Midas. He looked in a cupboard and found a long piece of red cloth. Carefully he tied the cloth round his head. He looked quite strange, but no one could see his ears. Under the cloth they felt hot, but his secret was safe.

Midas's secret

At breakfast everyone looked at the strange cloth on the King's head. No one said anything, however. In those days kings could do exactly as they liked. No one ever asked them about the way they behaved.

The Queen looked at him carefully when they were alone together. She could not understand why he was wearing a strange red cloth on his head. Midas said nothing. He did not care what she thought. He did not want her to know the truth.

For a long time Midas kept his secret. He slept with his head covered. He ate with his head covered. He even bathed with his head covered. Many men did the same. It became smart to wear something on your head all the time.

Sometimes Midas wore a tall gold hat. That was the best, because then his ears could stand up straight. Sometimes he folded them under a smaller hat. In the bath he covered them with a towel. No one — not even the Queen — saw the King without something on his head.

'Perhaps he is getting old and his hair is falling out,' the servants whispered. 'He is ashamed to let anyone see.' Midas heard, but he did not care. His secret was still safe.

Midas calls the barber

At last, however, Midas's hair became very long. 'I must have a haircut,' he said to himself, 'but I can't cut my own hair. My barber must cut it for me, and then he will discover my secret!'

Midas called his barber. 'I need a haircut,' he said. 'But before you start, you must promise me something. If anything surprises you when you are cutting my hair, you must promise to say nothing about it. You must tell no one. If you keep my secret I will reward you well. If you tell anyone you will die a terrible death.'

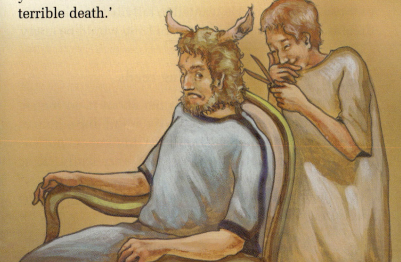

The barber did not understand, but he agreed. 'I promise I won't tell anyone,' he said. 'Now let me cut your hair.'

Midas took off his hat. The big brown ears sprang up on either side of his head. The barber wanted to laugh aloud, but he was too afraid of the King. He changed his laugh into a little cough, and started work.

When he had finished, he took the money that the King gave him. He promised once more to keep the King's secret. He folded the silly ears over the top of the King's head and put the hat on top of them.

'Remember,' said Midas. 'Don't tell anyone.'

'Your secret is safe with me, great King,' said the barber.

The barber tried very hard to keep his secret. He never said a word to anyone, but in his mind's eye he could see those foolish ears and the King's weak, silly face between them. He wished he could tell his family. Sometimes he thought about the donkey's ears, and laughed aloud.

'What's the matter?' his wife asked many times.

'Nothing, dear,' said the barber. At night he dreamt of those brown ears. He wanted to tell his wife about his dreams, but he was afraid that the King would be angry.

The whispering reeds

At last the barber could keep quiet about it no longer. He went down to the side of the river and dug a hole in the ground. Then he got down on his knees, put his mouth near the hole and whispered very softly, 'King Midas has donkey's ears.'

At once he felt better. 'I've kept my promise,' he said. 'I haven't told anyone.'

He filled up the hole with earth and stones and went home.

Spring came to Midas's kingdom. New leaves grew on the trees and fresh young reeds grew by the side of the river. The wind blew through the reeds. 'Sh-sh,' said the reeds. All except one little group of reeds near King Midas's palace. They whispered, 'King Midas has donkey's ears! King Midas has donkey's ears!'

A fisherman was sitting on the bank hoping to catch a fish. He heard the whispering reeds. He hurried home and told his family what he had heard. Soon the whole kingdom knew the King's secret. The barber escaped to another country but the King really could not blame the barber. He never told the secret to anyone, did he?

4
THESEUS AND THE MINOTAUR

The animal in the labyrinth

Not far from Greece is the island of Crete. Once there was a king of the island called Minos, who had a very strange and dangerous animal. It was called the Minotaur, after its master. The bottom half of its body was human. The rest of it, however, was like a great black animal called a bull.

Minos had a clever servant, Daedalus, who built a home for the Minotaur. This was called the labyrinth. Daedalus built it under the ground. There were hundreds of twisting, turning paths that led to an open space in the centre where the terrible Minotaur lived.

The Minotaur's favourite food was human meat, and Minos fed it every day on prisoners. He just pushed them through the gates of the labyrinth. Once inside, they were lost. There were so many paths going in

so many different directions that no one could ever find their way out. Sooner or later they reached the centre, and the Minotaur had a feast.

King Minos was the father of a baby boy. Minos loved his child very much and took great care of him. The young prince grew tall, strong and clever. Everyone liked him.

Aegeus and Theseus

At about the same time, in Greece, there was a prince called Aegeus who met a pretty girl and fell in love with her. They had a baby boy and named him Theseus. But when Theseus was only a few months old, Aegeus's father died.

Aegeus had to go to his father's kingdom, the city of Athens. He had to leave his wife and his little son behind. Before he went, however, he dug a hole in the ground. He put his sword in it and covered the place with a heavy, flat stone.

'My dear,' he said to Theseus's mother, 'when our son is big and strong, bring him to this place. Let him lift the stone and take my sword. As soon as he can get it for himself it will belong to him. Then he must go to Athens to find me.'

He kissed her goodbye and started on the long road to Athens.

The son of Minos goes to Athens

Every year the people of Athens had a special holiday. All the young men of Greece and the islands nearby met there. They took part in many different games and contests. Everyone wanted to join in the feasting and fun. Minos's son begged his father to let him travel to Athens too. Minos was not sure.

'You are my son,' he told the young prince. 'What if something happens to you? What will I do then?'

'Oh, Father, nothing can happen to me!' cried the young man. 'I just want to go to Athens for the games and contests, like all the other people. Please say yes, Father! Please!'

With a heavy heart Minos agreed. He and his little daughter, Ariadne, wished him good luck and waved goodbye.

Before long everyone in Athens knew and liked the Prince of Crete. He did very well in all the contests, but he never boasted about his skill. Everyone liked him, except King Aegeus. The King was very jealous of the young stranger.

One night, when the Prince was on his way back to Crete, King Aegeus sent some men after him. They killed the young prince and hid his body in the woods.

Every day Minos waited on the harbour wall for his son's ship. It returned without him.

The people of Athens were sad, too. They did not know what had happened to the young prince. They only knew that he was lost. Only King Aegeus knew the truth.

A few days after this, Aegeus's own son, Theseus, arrived in Athens.

Theseus arrives

For Theseus this was the happy end of a long and difficult journey. It all began on the day when he lifted the heavy stone. He took the sword from under it. Then he kissed his mother goodbye.

Many things happened to him on the long road to Athens. The road passed through hills where dangerous wild animals lived. There were also robbers and people who killed any strangers that came along. They all tried to fight him, and Theseus beat every one of them.

He arrived in Athens and Aegeus knew him at once. 'My son has come! We must have a feast!' the King shouted. He opened the gates of his palace to all the people. There was feasting and fun for several days. Wine poured from the palace fountains and there was free food for everyone. The people of Athens forgot the Prince of Crete and greeted their own young prince.

In Crete, Minos was still waiting for his son to return. At last some of Minos's soldiers found the boy lying dead in the woods not far from Athens. They sent messengers to Minos. The King told them to bring his son's body home, and he ordered a great funeral. He was very angry.

'Those people of Athens killed my son,' he said to himself. 'I shall punish them for this!' He sailed across the sea to Athens with a large army. Minos was going to attack the city.

Surrender!

Minos reached Athens with his army. Of course, the gates were closed and the walls were well guarded. Aegeus was waiting for them.

This did not frighten Minos, however. He and his men had plenty of food. They also had plenty of time. Outside the city walls they lit fires and began to cook their supper. 'All we have to do,' said King Minos to his officers, 'is wait here patiently. Soon Athens will be ours.'

The officers knew the King was right. Food for the people of Athens came from the farms outside the city.

Minos and his men stopped the farmers from going into Athens. No one could go into the city. No one could leave it without becoming a prisoner. In a week or two everyone in Athens was hungry. Soon children and old people became weak and ill. A few people died.

'They will surrender soon,' Minos told his men.

They saw their leader's cold, angry face. 'His son's death has changed him,' they whispered to each other. 'His heart has become hard.'

It hurt Aegeus to see his people so weak and ill. 'We must surrender,' he said at last to his wise men. 'I am too sad to let this continue.' He sent a messenger to the King of Crete. In his message Aegeus said he would surrender. He asked Minos to be kind to his poor people.

Minos read the message, and he laughed. It was a cold, cruel laugh. 'Kind!' he said. 'What kindness did the people of Athens show towards my son?'

The messenger came back to Athens with a white face and shaking hands. 'Great King,' he said to Aegeus, 'King Minos will leave our city if you promise him something.'

'I'll promise anything! Anything!' cried Aegeus.

Food for the Minotaur

'Every year you must send seven young men and seven young girls to Crete. There, Minos will give them to the Minotaur.'

King Aegeus gave a great cry. 'How can I allow this?' he cried. The wise men of the city said, 'Do you want *all* your people to die of hunger, great King? If you agree to what Minos asks, only a few will die.'

With a heavy heart King Aegeus agreed. The people of Athens chose their young people. It was a sad business. The wise men put small black and white balls into a large iron pot. Each boy took a ball out of the pot. If it was white, he was safe but only for one year. There were seven black balls. If a boy took a black ball, then he was one of the seven who had to go to Crete. The families watched in hope and fear.

Then it was the girls' turn to stand around the iron pot. Seven black balls; seven crying mothers. Fourteen sad people went away with King Minos to their death.

The next year the same terrible thing happened, and the year after that. The people of Athens were very unhappy and ashamed, but they were afraid of King Minos. They could not break their promise. The next year after that, however, Prince Theseus stepped forward.

Theseus goes to Crete

'Give me a black ball!' he said to the wise men. 'I am not going to let my friends go to their death without me. I shall try to kill the Minotaur and make our country free. If I fail, I shall be proud to die with my friends.'

'Don't go, Theseus!' begged the King. 'You are my son. Don't leave your poor father alone!'

'What about all the other parents?' said Theseus. 'No, Father, this cannot continue. I have to do something about it. If I don't, all the parents in Athens will live in fear. I must try to kill the Minotaur.'

A ship with black sails waited in the harbour. King Aegeus stood with the other parents on the harbour wall and waved goodbye. In his heart he was very sad. His son and the other young men and women were going to a cruel death. He would never see his son again. Now he understood how King Minos felt, and he cried.

Theseus saw his father crying. 'Don't be sad!' he called. 'I shall kill the Minotaur. Watch for this ship. When I come back I shall take down the black sails, and put up white ones. When you see the white sails, you will know I am safe and well.'

'I shall watch every day,' cried Aegeus. 'Goodbye, my dear son and good luck!'

Ariadne

Theseus was cheerful all through the journey to Crete. The others almost believed that he would kill the Minotaur. They reached the island and were taken to see King Minos. The King saw their white, frightened faces. For a moment he was sorry for them, and he was sorry for their parents, too. Then he thought of his own dead boy. All kindness left his heart.

His daughter, Ariadne, stood beside him. She was a beautiful girl with a kind, gentle heart. She saw the boys and girls and she thought of the dark labyrinth. She thought of the cruel Minotaur and tears filled her eyes.

King Minos saw Theseus and his eyes shone. 'This is the young prince of Athens!' he said.

Theseus stepped forward. 'I am Theseus, son of Aegeus,' he said. 'Great King, please let my companions sleep in peace in the palace yard tonight. They are tired after the journey. Let me enter the labyrinth alone. The others can follow me in the morning.'

'So the Prince is proud!' said Minos. 'He wishes to die alone. Very well, Prince Theseus, I will grant your wish.'

Ariadne was looking at the brave young prince. Her cheeks were pink and her heart was beating quickly. Her eyes shone with love. 'I *won't* let him die!' she said to herself. 'There must be a way to save him.'

'Father,' she said aloud, 'let me take the Prince to the labyrinth tonight. He is a king's son, and I am a king's daughter. I am the right person to do it.'

To the labyrinth

King Minos agreed. When it was dark Ariadne led Theseus to the gates of the labyrinth. It was a clear night. The bright full moon shone and a light wind was blowing. They reached the gate of the labyrinth.

'Prince Theseus,' said Ariadne, 'my heart is sad for you. You are brave and strong, and your sword is sharp. Why can't you kill the Minotaur tonight, and escape

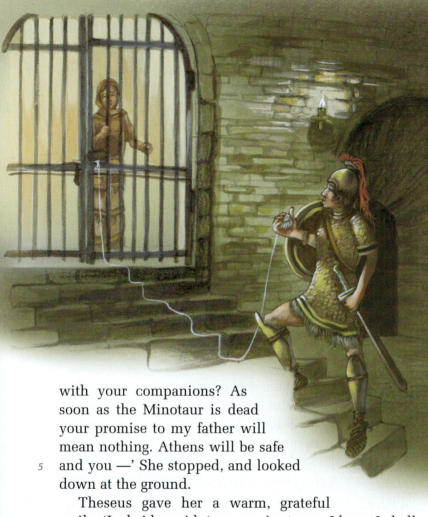

with your companions? As soon as the Minotaur is dead your promise to my father will mean nothing. Athens will be safe and you —' She stopped, and looked down at the ground.

Theseus gave her a warm, grateful smile. 'Lady,' he said, 'my arm is strong. I hope I shall kill the Minotaur. Then my companions will be able to escape. But I shall have to stay behind. You see, I shall never find my way out of the labyrinth. Everyone says it cannot be done.'

'It can be done,' whispered Ariadne. She gave him a ball of thin, strong thread. 'Fasten one end of this to the gate. Hold the ball in your right hand. When you have killed the Minotaur, you must follow the thread back. Roll it up as you go along. It may save your life!'

'Thank you a thousand times!' breathed Theseus. He kissed her and touched her hand. He dried the tears on her cheeks. Then he tied the thread to the gate and entered the labyrinth.

Saved by a thread

He followed the strange, twisted path that led to the Minotaur. It was dark and quiet. Soon Theseus could smell the Minotaur's hot breath. The smell grew stronger. Then he heard heavy breathing.

A black shape lay in front of him. It was darker than the darkness around him. The great black sides of the Minotaur moved like the sea with the beating of its great black heart. It was asleep. It was not waiting for food. That usually came in the morning. It was dreaming of soft, sweet young girls.

Very quietly Theseus crept up to the Minotaur. With one blow of his sword he cut off its head. The hot black blood poured out and boiled on the ground at Theseus's feet. He stepped back quickly. Then he felt for the thread in the darkness, and followed it.

He followed that thread through every dark twist and turn of the mysterious labyrinth. He rolled it up, and the ball of thread grew bigger.

The journey seemed to last for ever. For a while he thought that something was wrong. He was lost in the dark. Every bone in his body ached. His heart was beating like a frightened bird. 'I'll never get out of here,' he thought. But he continued to wind up the thread.

At last he saw the moon. The end of the thread was still tied to the gate. He had found his way back.

And there stood Ariadne! She had brought some food with her, and some water. He ran to her and took her in his arms. He kissed her and thanked her again and again. Then he told her his story while he ate and drank.

Escape!

'And now I must sleep,' he said at last.

'No, Prince Theseus!' said Ariadne. 'You must escape now! Wake your companions and tell them the good news. Then sail away before my father wakes.'

'And leave you behind?' said Theseus. 'What will your father do to you? Do you think he will reward you for your part in our escape? No, Ariadne, I'm taking you with me. You have saved my life, and I love you with all my heart. Come back to Athens and be my wife!'

'I fell in love with you the moment I saw you,' breathed Ariadne. 'I will go with you but we must hurry! Wake your friends before it is too late!'

Theseus woke up the others and took them out of Minos's palace. They were still rubbing their eyes as he led them down to the harbour. They sang and shouted as they sailed back to Athens.

They forgot one thing. They forgot to take down the black sails. They were all so happy that they never thought about King Aegeus on the harbour wall.

He stood and watched for his son's ship. At last he saw a dark shape in the distance. It came nearer, and he saw the black sails. He thought his son had been killed by the Minotaur. With a cry he threw himself into the sea and drowned.

Ever since then, the sea near Athens has been called the Aegean Sea, after him. Theseus became King of Athens and Ariadne was his queen. Athens was free, and Theseus ruled over the city for many happy years.

5
THE WONDERFUL WINGS

A clever artist

Long ago, in the city of Athens, there lived a man named Daedalus. He was the cleverest artist in the city. He made wonderful statues and he could also build lovely houses and temples. All the rich men of Athens asked Daedalus to build palaces for them. He filled them with statues and fountains and other beautiful things.

Not far from Athens was the island of Crete. Minos was King of Crete and he heard about Daedalus's skill. He had a strange animal called the Minotaur. This was a very dangerous animal, and Minos needed a safe place for it. He asked Daedalus to help him.

Daedalus built the labyrinth, and the Minotaur lived there — until Theseus killed it. The labyrinth was Daedalus's greatest piece of work. He was very proud of it. Minos was very pleased with it, too, and he gave Daedalus a large reward.

'Remember,' he told Daedalus, 'come to Crete any time you like. You will always be welcome here.'

Daedalus thanked the King and went back to Athens.

Icarus and Perdix

Daedalus's wife was dead. He looked after his little son Icarus alone. Icarus could not help his father. He was too young, but Daedalus had another person to help him. This was his nephew, Perdix. Perdix's parents were dead and his uncle Daedalus took care of him.

Perdix was a clever, eager boy. He wanted to be as skilful as his uncle. He listened carefully to every word Daedalus said. He copied everything carefully. Daedalus was glad to have such a good pupil. He taught Perdix everything he knew. He was a good teacher as well as a clever artist. Soon the boy was making wonderful things.

Perdix was soon as skilful as Daedalus. He used his skill in new and clever ways.

'One day,' the people of Athens said, 'Perdix will be a better artist than his uncle.'

Daedalus was pleased and proud at first. Then he began to feel hurt and jealous. He began to think that his pupil might be greater than he was. He could not bear that. All his love for his nephew turned to hate.

The cliff

One evening he asked Perdix to walk with him by the seashore. It was a beautiful, quiet summer evening. The sun was going down into the dark blue sea. Daedalus led Perdix to the top of a hill, near the sea. The side of the hill nearest the sea went straight down into the water. It was a cliff. Together Daedalus and Perdix stood at the top of the cliff and looked down.

'The sea is a beautiful blue, Uncle,' said Perdix. 'I want to make curtains in exactly that colour. I shall hang them in the temple of Athene. Don't you think they will look wonderful?'

He talked and talked about his work, and his plans for the future. He did not see the black anger in his uncle's eyes. Suddenly Daedalus stepped back a little. He gave the boy a hard push. Perdix found himself falling over the cliff edge. He tried to catch hold of some grass, but it tore away in his hands. With a cry he fell down, down towards the rocks at the bottom of the cliff.

He did not die, however. The goddess Minerva heard his cry. She knew Perdix well and loved him for his skill. She changed him into a small brown bird. He opened his wings and flew away over the sea.

The escape to Crete

Daedalus knew that he was in trouble. 'If anyone hears about this,' he said to himself, 'they will kill me. I must run away at once.'

He put a few things in an old bag. Then he woke his little son. 'Come on, Icarus,' he said, 'we must leave at once.'

'What's the matter?' asked Icarus. He was still sleepy. He rubbed his eyes and looked up into his father's face.

'We must leave Athens at once. If we don't, we shall be in great danger. Put your clothes on and follow me quietly!'

They went down to the harbour. There they climbed into a little fishing boat. Icarus watched his father pull up the sail. Daedalus was as good at sailing as he was at everything else.

'Where are we going, Father?' asked Icarus.

'To Crete, son. King Minos will make us welcome. He is my friend and will give me work, but we must go quickly.'

The prisoners

Minos remembered Daedalus's work on the labyrinth. He was glad to see him. He gave Daedalus a place to work in and kept him very busy. Daedalus did some very good work for the King.

But one day Daedalus argued with the King. It was not an important matter. Minos wanted some small thing, and Daedalus said he must wait. Minos was angry and Daedalus was too proud to ask the King's pardon. Trouble often starts in small ways.

'I'll teach *you* a lesson!' Minos shouted. 'Guards! Throw this man into prison. I will see him when he has learnt not to be so rude.'

They locked Daedalus and little Icarus in a room at the top of a tall building. There Daedalus and his son lived for several weeks. Every day Icarus watched the birds that flew past his window.

'I wish we could fly like that, Father,' he said. 'Then we could fly away; we would be free!'

Daedalus said nothing. But already he had an idea. As the days went by that idea grew. He watched the birds and studied the way they flew.

One night Daedalus began to make some wings.

He took birds' feathers of different sizes. He stuck them to some thin pieces of wood with wax. He used hundreds of feathers. At last the work was finished. There were two pairs of wings, a small pair and a large pair. The sun was just rising as Daedalus stood back and looked at his work.

Flying away

'Wake up, Icarus!' he said. 'We are going to fly like the birds. Won't that be fun?'

Carefully he fastened the small pair of wings to Icarus's back. Then he put on his own wings. He moved his arms up and down a few times. The wings seemed to work very well. Would they carry his weight? He could not be sure.

'Follow me, son,' he said, 'and do exactly what I tell you. Don't fly too low. If you do, the water may wet your wings. Then you will drop into the sea and drown. Do not fly too high either. I have stuck the feathers of your wings with wax. If you fly too high, the heat of the sun will melt the wax. So take care!'

He kissed his little son. He climbed up to the window and stood there for a moment. Then he took a deep breath and threw himself into space.

For a moment he thought he was going to crash to the ground. Then he spread his arms out wide. The great wings opened. He was flying! He called out to Icarus.

'Jump, son, and spread out your arms. The wings will hold you up.' Icarus closed his eyes and jumped. The wings opened wide. He was flying, too! It was a wonderful feeling. He joined his father. Together they looked down at their prison. It looked very far away.

Off to Sicily

A guard was standing on the palace wall. He saw them and pointed up at them. To Daedalus and Icarus he looked like a toy soldier.

'Get your bows!' the officer of the guard shouted. 'Shoot them before they can get away!' The soldiers ran about and shot at the two escaped prisoners, but Daedalus and Icarus were too high up, and too far away. Daedalus just laughed. They were quite safe.

'Where are we going, Father?' asked Icarus.

'Sicily, I hope. I have friends there. We shall be safe.'

On and on they flew, over land and sea. Some people below watched them. 'Look!' they cried, 'two gods are flying here from heaven. Quick! Get down on your knees and pray!'

A fisherman thought they were two big birds. He tried to shoot them but they were too quick for him.

The sun rose higher in the sky. Icarus was becoming quite clever at flying. He practised diving down towards the sea. It was very exciting but he always remembered his father's words. He opened his wings before he came too near the water. He did not want to wet his wings.

Soon, however, he began to feel very brave and sure of himself. He saw birds flying far above him, above the clouds. He wanted to join them in the clear blue sky. He looked quickly towards his father. Daedalus was flying along slowly and carefully. Every beat of his great wings was carrying him closer to Sicily.

Icarus opened his wings wide and flew up, up towards the hot white sun. He was so happy that he forgot the wax on his feathers.

The heat of the sun

The sun's fierce heat burned Icarus's face. Soon the wax around his feathers began to melt. One by one the feathers dropped from the wings. They fell like snow towards the sea. Icarus had nothing to hold him up. He began to fall! In his fear he cried out to his father.

Daedalus heard the boy's cries. He turned his head to look and he saw Icarus falling. He flew towards the boy as fast as he could. But he could not fly fast enough. Icarus hit the water and went below the waves.

Daedalus tore off his own wings and dived into the sea. He swam down until he found Icarus. He fought his way up again with Icarus in his arms. He looked about for land. There was an island in the distance. Daedalus held Icarus and swam on his back towards the shore. He prayed all the time. He made many promises to the gods. 'Just let Icarus live,' he begged. 'I'll never ask you for anything else.'

At last he felt sand and stones under his feet. He stood up and carried his son towards the island. Icarus was still and cold. Daedalus breathed into the boy's mouth. He moved the stiff little arms up and down. But it was no good. Icarus was dead.

The Icarian Sea

With a heavy heart, Daedalus dug a hole in the ground, and placed the body of the dead boy in it. He got down on his knees there and prayed. As he prayed he heard a bird calling above his head. He looked up and saw a small brown bird.

'Perdix! Remember Perdix!' the bird seemed to say. Daedalus remembered his poor young nephew. 'So this is how the gods have punished me for the bad thing that I did,' he said to himself. 'Well, I deserved it.'

For a long time after that, the island was called Icarus. The sea where the boy drowned was called the Icarian Sea.

6
PLUTO AND PERSEPHONE

The daughter of Ceres

Long ago, all the seasons were the same. It was never really cold and the leaves never fell from the trees. The whole earth was fresh and green all the year.

The goddess Ceres took care of the land that people used for farming, and the plants that they grew on it. She was tall and golden like the crops in summer. She was warm and kind, and the farmers loved her. They prayed to her before they planted their seeds. Ceres rewarded them so that the crops grew well every year. There was peace and plenty everywhere.

Ceres had a daughter called Persephone. If Ceres was like the summer, Persephone was like the spring. Her cheeks were pink and white like the flowers on the fruit trees. Her eyes were as blue as April skies. Her laugh was like clear, cold streams. Everyone loved her.

Persephone spent the long, bright days in the fields. Sometimes she helped her mother. Sometimes she sang and danced with the young nymphs.

Deep down under the Earth, there lived a dark, old god called Pluto. He ruled the kingdom of the dead. He had no one to live with him in his dark home. He tried to find a goddess or nymph to live with him. He said he would give them gold and jewels, but no one wanted to leave the bright light of the sun behind. So Pluto became lonelier and lonelier. He thought about his life and how he could change it.

Sometimes the sound of Persephone's songs and laughter reached Pluto in his dark palace. That made him sadder and lonelier than ever.

The dark chariot

At last he knew that he had to do something about his unhappy life. He fastened his horses to his dark chariot. He shook the reins.

'Up!' he ordered. The two great black horses raced up towards the Earth.

Persephone was playing with a group of nymphs. They had flowers in their hands, and they were chasing her. They threw flowers at her, and she pretended to cry and run away. It was quite a silly game, but they were all enjoying it very much. Persephone was helpless with laughter. Her cheeks were pink and her eyes shone.

Suddenly the ground shook. A hole opened at her feet. Dark clouds of black smoke came out of the hole. Persephone heard the noise of horses' hoofs. With a flash of lightning and a great crash of thunder Pluto's dark chariot appeared.

The laughter died on her lips. The nymphs screamed with fright and picked up their skirts and ran. Persephone turned to run too, but Pluto reached out and caught her arm.

'Not so fast, my pretty one,' he said. He looked at her beautiful, frightened face and his heart was filled with love. 'You shall be my queen,' he said. 'I will give you all my gold and jewels. You shall rule the land of the dead with me.'

Pluto drives away

As he spoke, Pluto felt very sad. He knew that Persephone would never agree to go with him. He had to *make* her go. He held her arm more tightly.

The nymphs had run away. They were too frightened to help Persephone. They hid in the woods and streams.

Pluto picked Persephone up in his arms and lifted her into the chariot. He had to get away at once. He did not want Ceres to see him. He shook the reins and shouted to his horses. The chariot went very fast. Persephone shut her eyes and held on to the sides of the chariot.

Pluto reached a river. He got ready to drive his horses through the water. But the nymph of the river saw Persephone. She made the river water rise up. Great waves appeared and Pluto's horses were afraid. Pluto saw that they could not go that way. But he could not turn back either; there was no time to lose. He shouted, 'Open!' and pointed at the ground. At once a great hole appeared in front of him. Horses and chariot dived down into the darkness. Pluto was returning to his kingdom.

The lost belt

Persephone saw the nymph of the river. She knew the nymph was trying to help her. 'Tell my mother!' Persephone cried. She took off her belt and threw it into the water.

Pluto put his big hand over Persephone's mouth. 'Quiet!' he ordered. The ground closed over their heads, and the chariot drove on into the darkness of Pluto's kingdom.

That evening Ceres came home. Persephone usually ran to greet her. This time, however, everything was quiet.

'She's hiding somewhere,' thought Ceres. 'She will jump out in a moment, and surprise me.'

'I'm coming to find you!' she called aloud. There was no answer. Ceres looked all over the house. It was empty. Then Ceres became frightened. She lit a torch and went out to look for Persephone. She looked for her all night. When morning came, she still had not found her lovely daughter.

Ceres forgot her duties. She did not listen to the prayers of the people. She spent every minute of every day looking for her lost child. The sun stopped shining, and the sky turned dark and cold. The crops stopped growing. The ground was dry and dead. The leaves fell from the trees. People all over the world were hungry. Some died of hunger, and some died because they were so cold.

The nymph speaks

The people prayed to Ceres. They begged her to be their friend again. 'We need you!' they said. 'Come back to us and make our fields green again.'

Ceres heard their prayers, but she shook her head sadly. She could not think of anything except her lost daughter.

A few days later, she was standing sadly by a river when a little wave rose up. It touched her foot. She looked down and saw a belt at her feet.

'Thank you,' breathed Ceres. She picked up the belt. It was her daughter's belt; she was sure of that. She looked at it with tears in her eyes.

Then water began to come up out of the ground in front of her. Ceres thought that the sound of the water was like someone speaking. She listened carefully, and heard the words, 'I am the nymph of this fountain. I have come up from the centre of the earth. Great Ceres, I have seen your daughter. She was sitting on a golden chair beside King Pluto. She was wearing many jewels but her cheeks were thin and white and her eyes were sad. Save her, Ceres, or she will die.'

Ceres goes to Jupiter

Ceres thanked the nymph. She hurried to Mount Olympus, the greatest of all mountains, and the home of the gods. She asked to speak to Jupiter. He was the father and king of all the gods. He was wise and good. Ceres was sure he would help her.

'I know where my daughter is,' she told him. 'She is a prisoner of the god Pluto, in the kingdom of the dead. Please order Pluto to give her back to me. Then the Earth will be green again and my people will be happy.'

Jupiter sat and thought for a moment. 'Has she eaten anything in Pluto's kingdom?' he asked. 'If she has, she belongs to him. If she has not, I shall be able to save her.'

Jupiter sent a messenger to Pluto, and ordered him to come to Mount Olympus. The dark god appeared in a cloud of smoke. 'Please bring Persephone to me,' Jupiter ordered.

'I won't,' said Pluto.

Jupiter gave him an angry look.

'Get her, before I throw lightning at you!' he roared. Pluto knew all about Jupiter's lightning. He went to fetch Persephone.

Ceres cried when she saw how thin and sad her daughter looked. The poor girl held her hand in front of her eyes. The light hurt her. Ceres ran to greet her, but Jupiter stopped her.

'Not yet,' he said. He turned to Persephone. 'Dear child,' he said, 'I want to return you to your mother. But I must do what is right for Pluto, too. Tell me, did you eat anything — anything at all — while you were in the kingdom of the dead?'

The apple

Persephone's eyes filled with tears. 'He said he would give me many things,' she said. 'He put wonderful food on golden dishes, and I refused everything. At last he brought a lovely red apple from my mother's own tree. I ate half of it. Look!' She held up a half-eaten apple. Ceres gave a cry of pain.

'She is mine!' roared Pluto.

'No!' begged Ceres. 'Please, Jupiter, help us.'

'Listen to me,' said Jupiter. 'I must do what is right for both of you; now hear my answer. Persephone has eaten half the apple, so she must be with Pluto for half the time. She must spend half of every year with him in the kingdom of the dead. The other half of the year, she may return to the world. Persephone, you may now spend six months with your mother. Pluto, come back in six months' time.'

Ceres kissed Jupiter's feet. Then she took her daughter in her arms. 'Come home, dear,' she said.

Pluto looked hard at them. 'My time will come,' he said with a bitter laugh. He jumped into his dark chariot and drove away.

And so that is how winter came to the Earth. Every year, at the end of summer, Persephone says goodbye to her mother and all her friends. She spends six months in the kingdom of the dead. Then the leaves fall from the trees. Nothing will grow in the fields and the Earth falls asleep. In spring, however, Persephone comes back. The Earth wakes from its winter sleep, the trees turn green and everyone is happy.

7
A WONDERFUL MUSICIAN

Orpheus and Eurydice

Orpheus lived in Greece a long time ago. He was a most wonderful musician. When he played his lyre the birds would stop singing and listen to his beautiful music. When he sang, the nymphs and satyrs always came out of the woods. They would stand round Orpheus and beg him to continue. Orpheus's music made everyone forget their sad, bitter and wicked thoughts. It made everyone feel happy and good.

Orpheus had a wife called Eurydice. He loved her very much. He made up many of his best songs for her. She was fresh and young and lovely, and they made each other very happy.

One day Eurydice was out in the fields picking flowers with several other girls. Eurydice wanted to put the flowers in the bedroom to surprise her husband. Suddenly a snake crawled from under a rock. Before Eurydice could move away, it bit her foot. She gave a little cry and fell to the ground. Her companions ran to help her. They carried her home to Orpheus.

Eurydice dies

Orpheus did everything he could for her, but in a few hours she was dead. Orpheus was so sad. It was terrible to see him. He picked up his lyre and tried to play. The music was so low and sad that even the rocks and the trees began to cry. He tried to sing, but he could not.

The nymphs and satyrs were sad too. They loved Eurydice and they were sorry for Orpheus.

At last he could not bear his lonely life any longer. He decided to go and look for Eurydice in the kingdom of the dead. This was a very dangerous thing to do.

'If I do it, we shall be together in life,' he said. 'If I fail, then I shall die. Pluto will take me to her, and we shall be together in death. I must go now; I cannot live without her.'

He went to the river of death. There a dark boatman waited. His job was to take the spirits of the dead people across the river into the dark kingdom.

'Boatman!' called Orpheus. 'I am looking for my wife. Will you take me across the river?'

'This ferry is for the spirits of the dead,' the boatman replied. 'I cannot take you.'

Orpheus made no answer. He picked up his lyre and began to play. He sang a long, sweet, sad song.

The boatman listened. His cold, hard heart seemed to melt. Tears ran down his cheeks. 'I will take you, but it is a dangerous place,' he said.

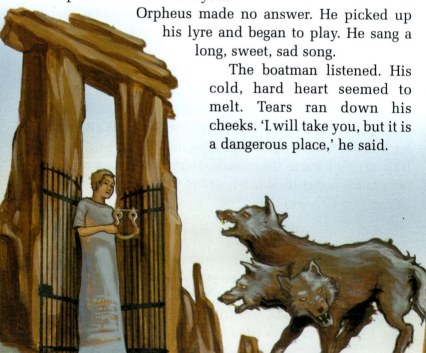

The terrible dog

They reached the far bank of the river of death. Orpheus climbed out and looked around him. He was at the gate of the dark kingdom. There stood a fierce dog. It was as big as a horse, and it had three heads. Each head had a pair of fire-red eyes and a large number of sharp yellow teeth.

The dog saw Orpheus and began to show all its teeth. It was ready to attack Orpheus and tear him to pieces. However, Orpheus picked up his lyre and began to play. The music was soft and gentle. The dog lay down on its back and waved its legs in the air. Orpheus scratched the dog under all three hairy chins. It shut its six eyes and licked his fingers.

'You're a nice old dog,' said Orpheus. 'You'll let me go through the gate, won't you?' The dog waved its tail and licked Orpheus again. With shaking hands the musician opened the gate. A dark, twisting path led to the palace of the dark god, Pluto. Orpheus followed it for many miles.

The dark god

At last Orpheus came into an open space. In front of him was a palace. The great doors were open wide. Orpheus walked in and found himself in a wide hall. There sat Pluto with his young wife, Persephone, at his side.

'What are *you* doing here?' roared Pluto when he saw Orpheus. 'No living man enters my halls. There must be some mistake. Who sent you here? Tell me, and I will punish him.'

'There is no mistake,' said Orpheus. 'I came here to look for my wife, Eurydice. A snake bit her and she died. It was only a few days ago but it seems like years. Great Pluto, I cannot live without her. Let me take her home with me now.'

Pluto looked at Persephone and whispered something. The young goddess whispered something back. She seemed to want her husband to grant Orpheus's wish, but the dark god shook his head.

Then Orpheus took up his lyre and began to play it. He sang about his love for Eurydice. He sang about her cruel death. He sang about his lonely life since then. The god's dark eyes became bright with tears. Persephone hid her lovely face in her hands and cried. The spirits of the dead came to listen, and they cried too.

Pluto grants Orpheus's prayer

When Orpheus had finished, Pluto spoke. 'Very well,' he said, 'I will grant your prayer. You can take your wife home now.' He called to two of the spirits. 'Bring Eurydice here.' Orpheus went down on his knees and kissed the dark god's feet.

'Wait,' said Pluto. 'Just one thing. You must not look back at your wife until you have passed through my gates. If you look back, she will be lost for ever.'

'Oh, thank you!' cried Orpheus. 'I promise.'

They brought Eurydice to him. She was very thin and her skin was white, but she knew him, and she smiled and held out her hands to him. Persephone kissed her goodbye. Then Orpheus and Eurydice began their dangerous journey.

They went along the dark twisting path. Orpheus could see the gates a few steps in front of him. But was Eurydice still following him? He could not be sure.

'Just one look,' he thought. 'Pluto will never know. I can't go through the gates without her!' He turned his head and gave one quick look. Eurydice was only a few steps behind. As soon as he looked, she stopped. She put out her arms to him. She opened her mouth to speak, but no sound came out.

'Eurydice, follow me!' cried Orpheus. 'We are almost there. Only a few more steps.'

Very sadly she shook her head. She became thinner and smaller; then she was gone.

Orpheus returns to Earth

Orpheus went out through the gate. The terrible dog licked his hand and wanted to play. Orpheus cried. He went to the river and asked the boatman to help him. When he had told his story, the boatman just shook his head.

'Pluto will never grant your prayer a second time,' he said. 'Go home, young man, and try to forget the past.'

For seven days and nights Orpheus sat by the river without food or sleep. At last he returned to the green Earth. He went up on to a high mountain. He lived a sad, lonely life there. He lived with the birds, the trees and the wild animals. If he could not have Eurydice, he did not want any other human with him.

He still played and sang. Musicians are like birds; they cannot stop singing, even when they are sad. But his songs were all sad songs.

The dancing women

One day, however, Orpheus was walking on the mountain when he met a group of women. They were all singing and dancing. When they saw his lyre, they shouted to him.

'Hello! Come and play us a song!' Orpheus shook his head.

'Come on. Let's have something cheerful!' they shouted. They spoke loudly and roughly and their breath smelt of wine. Orpheus tried to explain, but they would not listen.

At last the women became angry. They threw stones at him. One of them hit Orpheus on the side of the head. He fell to the ground. The women laughed and shouted and they threw more and more stones. At last he lay on the ground, dying, with his lyre beside him.

They threw the musician into the river. As he went down the river his last words were, 'Eurydice! Eurydice!'

Everything — the trees, the birds, the animals, even the rocks — felt sad. The wood nymphs and water nymphs forgot their games and cried for the sweet singer.

They were wrong to be sad. Orpheus reached the river of death with a light heart. The boatman welcomed him and took him across the river. The fierce dog with three heads licked his hand to greet him. At the gate stood Eurydice. He ran forward to meet his dear wife. She threw her arms around his neck. Orpheus and Eurydice were together again, and nothing could separate them.

8
THE GOLDEN CHARIOT OF THE SUN

Phaeton's secret

Once, in Greece, there was a boy who had never seen his father. The boy's name was Phaeton. He lived with his mother in a small house not far from Athens.

One day Phaeton asked his mother about his father. 'Where is my father?' he asked. 'Who is he? Is he dead? Why doesn't he live here with us? All my friends have their fathers living with them, so why can't I? It really makes me very unhappy to have no father.'

Phaeton's mother knew that the time had come to tell her son the truth. She took his hands in hers, and made him sit down next to her. She looked into his eyes and said, 'Phaeton, I will tell you everything about your father, but you must promise not to tell anyone else. This is a secret that only you and I can know about.'

Phaeton promised. 'I will never tell anyone, Mother,' he said.

'Your father is not dead,' his mother said. 'And you can be sure that he loves us very much. But he cannot stay with us because of his work. He has to do this work every day. Every day he has to travel far, far away from Athens. You see, my child, your father is Apollo, the sun-god.'

Phaeton was very surprised. He thought about what his mother had told him. He began to feel very happy and very proud.

'My father is the sun-god,' he said. 'So that means I see my father nearly every day, high in the sky above our house.'

'That's right,' said his mother. 'Every morning it is your father who drives the sun-chariot out of the mountains in the east. He takes it above the clouds, almost up to heaven, where the gods and goddesses live. Then he drives carefully back down again to the sea in the west. Every night he returns to his palace, and he must be up very early the next morning to do his work all over again. So do you understand now why your father cannot live with us?'

'I do, Mother,' said the boy, but Phaeton had already stopped thinking about why his father did not live at home. Now he was thinking about his father flying across the sky in the sun-chariot. What must it be like to do that? What was it like, high up there above the clouds? Would you be able to see all the countries in the world? Could you see all the way across the sea to Africa? If you were in the sun-chariot and looked up, could you see the great palaces and temples and beautiful gardens of the gods in heaven? It must be very exciting, to do work like that.

Phaeton visits Apollo

Phaeton was not an unhappy boy any more. He went around feeling very pleased with himself. For many days he had only one thought in his head, 'My father is Apollo, the sun-god.'

His friends could all see he was happy. They could not understand what had happened to him. What was making Phaeton look so very pleased? Had someone given him something? Was he going to leave them to go and live in another, more interesting place? They asked him many questions, but Phaeton kept his promise to his mother. He said nothing to anyone: except, of course, his best friend.

People often think that when they promise to keep a secret, it is all right to tell their best friend. Phaeton said to his best friend, 'I will tell you why I am so happy, if you promise never to tell anyone.' Phaeton's best friend promised. Then Phaeton's best friend went to *his* best friend and said, 'I will tell you why Phaeton is so happy if you promise never to tell anyone.' Of course, that person promised, and then went to tell *his* best friend.

Everyone is someone's best friend, so before long everyone knew Phaeton's secret. And soon after that everyone was laughing about it. How could Phaeton be the son of Apollo? That was much too foolish to be true.

Phaeton became very angry. He believed what his mother had told him. He knew he was Apollo's son. But how could he get his friends to believe him? There seemed only one thing to do. That was to go to his father, Apollo, and ask for his help. Perhaps his father would take him up in the sun-chariot. Perhaps Apollo would let him drive the sun-chariot all by himself. Then, when his friends saw him up in the sky, they would have to believe him.

'I must go and see my father, Apollo,' Phaeton said to his mother. 'Please tell me which way to go.'

'Your father's palace is on the far side of a country which is a long way to the east of our country,' his mother said. 'The name of that country is India. Go to India, then go across, further and further to the east, and in the end you will come to the sun-god's palace.'

Apollo's promise

It was a very long journey, but Phaeton had decided that he must see his father. It took him many months. Most of the way he walked. Sometimes he had to take a boat across a river, or a ship over the wide sea. If he was lucky, people sometimes gave him a ride on a donkey or a horse, but that did not happen often.

Then, one day, his long journey was almost finished. He stood at the bottom of a tall mountain. Everywhere in front of him, to his left and to his right, were other tall, steep mountains. He could not walk to the east any further. He had reached the end of the world.

At the top of one of the mountains, not far away, he could see a large, beautiful palace. The walls and the buildings inside were all shining with bright gold.

Phaeton knew that this must be the palace of the sun-god.

When he reached the palace he asked someone to take him to Apollo. Of course, the servants told him to wait until night-time. Apollo was never at home during the day. But when night came Apollo returned, and soon he and Phaeton had met and were talking to one another.

'Are you really my father?' Phaeton asked.

'I am,' said Apollo, and smiled happily at his son, 'and I am very pleased that you have come all this way to see me. Now, because you are my son, and because this is the first time we have met, I want to give you something. Tell me what you would like. It can be anything.'

Phaeton thought for a while. Then he said, 'What I would like is not a thing. It is something I want to do. I can only do it if you let me.'

'Anything, my son, I promise you. It can be anything you like.'

'I want you to let me drive the sun-chariot, by myself.'

Apollo stopped smiling. 'My son, you cannot do that. Only I, Apollo, can drive the sun-chariot. The chariot is large and heavy. Not even Jupiter, the great king of all the gods, can drive it. Once it is moving, it is very hard to stop it. The horses are the strongest horses anyone has ever seen. You will never be able to make them obey you. If I let you drive the sun-chariot I am afraid you will not drive it well, and that will be dangerous for everyone. Please, my son, ask for something else.'

But Phaeton would not change his mind, and Apollo had promised him anything he liked.

The sun-chariot

Early the next morning, Apollo took Phaeton to the chariot. When Phaeton saw it he became very excited. Never in his life had he seen such a beautiful chariot. It was much larger than he had thought. Even the wheels were almost twice as big as he was. It had two great wings, one on each side, and it was covered with gold and bright-coloured jewels. The four great black horses were very strong and excited about starting their journey. You could see that they wanted nothing better than to run as fast as they could for ever and ever.

Apollo tried to tell Phaeton all about driving the chariot. He showed him how to stand at the front of the chariot, and how to hold on to the reins. He told him the names of the horses, and how to call to each one to make it obey him. He told him about the road through the sky, which parts he must drive through as fast as possible, and which parts he must drive through slowly and carefully.

Phaeton seemed to be listening, but he did not listen well. All he could think about was driving that chariot up through the sky.

Phaeton's ride begins

Phaeton got on to the chariot, and took hold of the reins. The palace servants opened the great gates. In front of him he could see a road through the sky, going up high above the clouds. It was time to start.

He took the reins in his hands, and shouted 'Go!' as loudly as he could. The horses pulled. The great wheels began to turn. They were moving. Faster and faster they went, towards the palace gates. Phaeton felt himself falling backwards and he held on to the front of the chariot.

Then, suddenly, they were through the gates and up, out, into the air. The land seemed to fall away below them. Phaeton looked over the side of the chariot and could not believe his eyes. There, below him, were the hills and forests and rivers and villages and towns of India. He could see everything.

As the chariot climbed into the morning air it moved further and further away from the ground. Everything got smaller and smaller.

It drove into some clouds and for a while Phaeton could see nothing at all. Then it was out, above the clouds, climbing higher and higher into the dark blue sky towards heaven and the palaces of the gods.

The stars run away

By this time the chariot was going very fast. Phaeton began to think he should do something. Perhaps he should pull the reins back to make the horses go more slowly. He tried. Nothing happened. He shouted at the horses, 'Slow down, slow down! You are going too fast!' Nothing happened. 'I must call them by their names,' he said to himself. He could not remember their names. 'I will shout louder,' he thought to himself. 'That will stop them.' But it only made the horses run faster.

Soon the sun-chariot was higher than it had ever been before. When it reached the palaces of heaven it should have started going down, to the west, but it kept going up. It went up into the darkness, where there are only stars and a few very strange animals and people. Phaeton saw a large bear, and not far from it a smaller bear. He saw a long snake, sleeping near the north star. He saw a farmer, a hunter and his dog, a lion, an eagle, and a dangerous-looking insect, called a scorpion.

The sun-chariot was now far away from the world. The earth began to grow dark and cold. The people could not understand what was happening.

Up in the sky, the star-animals and star-people could not understand why everything was so warm and bright. What was the sun doing in their place? The farmer and the hunter ran to the north as fast as they could. The heat from the sun-chariot woke up the old sleeping snake, and made it very angry. The bears tried to climb down from the sky into the sea.

The world on fire

The bright light made the star-scorpion jump at the horses, and that frightened them very badly. This time the horses pulled the sun-chariot down towards the world. Phaeton tried to slow them, and make them go in the right direction, but nothing made any difference. The horses would not obey him. They ran this way and that, sometimes too far to the north, sometimes too far to the south, sometimes too high in the sky, and sometimes too low.

When the sun-chariot came close to the ground, the heat caused fires to start. The trees and grass began to burn. Houses burst into flames. Soon black smoke was rising into the air from the burning fields and forests. Whole cities were on fire. Large parts of the earth turned into dry, sandy deserts.

The heat warmed the water in the rivers and the seas. Soon the rivers began to dry up. The fish in the sea swam down to the lowest, darkest places to keep cool. Before long the people and the animals began to die. The whole world was in danger of coming to an end.

Phaeton's fall

Poor Phaeton looked this way and that. He looked at the Sun Palace, but he could not make the horses go back there. He looked to the west, but the horses would not go that way either. He looked down on the world and saw the terrible fires and the great clouds of black smoke. He knew now that his father had been right.

The chariot was much
too big for him to drive.
But there was nothing he
could do.

All the gods met together. They
could see that something had to be
done. If they did nothing their own palaces
would soon be burnt down, and there would be no
world left for them to live in. They called for Apollo,
who told them what had happened. He said he could
not do anything while Phaeton was still in the chariot.

Jupiter, the king of the gods, knew that there was
only one thing to do. It made him very sad, but nothing
else would work.

He walked to the top of his palace, the largest palace
in the heavens, and looked out. Down below him he
could see the sun-chariot, moving about this way and
that, with Phaeton holding on as tightly as he could.

Jupiter took a ball of lightning, and threw it straight at Phaeton. It hit the boy, and knocked him out of the chariot. Apollo was then able to fly from heaven down into his chariot, and, at last, drive it to its correct place in the sky.

Nothing could save poor Phaeton. He fell, far and fast, down through the sky, his long hair burning as he went. Some people saw him fall, and said that a star fell from heaven.

Phaeton fell into a river called the Eridanus. Some people think that that is the large river in the north of Italy which is now called the Po. For a long time they say that there was a stone at the side of the river. It showed people where Phaeton fell. They would come there and put flowers on the stone, to remember him.

QUESTIONS AND ACTIVITIES

1 The Golden Touch

Put the sentences in the right order.

1 Dionysus gave King Midas his wish. ☐
2 King Midas reached out to touch her. ☐
3 His lovely little daughter was alive again. ☐
4 Dionysus told him to go to the river to bathe. ☐
5 The King was happy because he thought he was very rich. ☐
6 After he had washed, nothing he touched turned to gold. ☐
7 Midas washed himself in the river. ☐
8 She turned into a beautiful gold statue. ☐
9 Then his daughter came to see him. ☐
10 Midas was so unhappy that he asked Dionysus to take back the golden touch. ☐

2 The First Spider

Put the words in brackets in the right order.

1 Arachne could make [pictures] [beautiful] [in cloth]

   Arachne could make _____.

2 People paid her [large amounts] [for her pictures] [of money]

   People paid her _____.

3 [she could make] [Minerva] [She said] [than the goddess] [better pictures]

_____.

4 [a beautiful picture] [made] [and Arachne] [both] [Minerva]

_____.

5 [the gods] [showed] [how foolish people] [disobeyed] [Minerva's picture]

_____.

6 [sometimes] [Arachne's picture] [make mistakes] [how the gods] [was about]

_____.

7 [Arachne's picture] [was] [than hers] [Minerva said that] [better]

_____.

8 [was angry,] [into a spider] [and she turned] [Arachne] [Minerva]

_____.

3 The Donkey's Ears

Fill in the gaps with the words from the box.

| barber | ears | music | secret |
| donkey | haircut | reeds | |

Two gods, Pan and Apollo, liked to play
(1) _music_ . King Midas said Pan plays better

than Apollo. This made Apollo angry. He turned the King's (2) _cars_ into the (3) _cars_ of a (4) _donkey_. Midas needed a (5) _haircut_, but he did not want anyone to know his (6) _secret_. He made the (7) _barber_ promise to say nothing. The (8) _barber_ kept his promise but he spoke the (9) _secret_ into a hole near the river. Later the (10) _ready_ near the hole whispered what the (11) _baber_ had said, and everyone knew the King's (12) _secret_.

4 Theseus and the Minotaur

Correct the underlined part of each sentence.

1 Aegeus ordered some men to kill the son of Minos, <u>King of Greece</u>.

2 After that some young people of Athens <u>were sent to Crete each week</u>.

3 They were put in the labyrinth, where <u>King Minos</u> ate them.

4 One year <u>Aegeus said he would go to Crete</u> with the other young people.

5 In Crete <u>he met Ariadne, Minos's wife</u>, who helped him.

6 Ariadne <u>took Theseus to the palace</u> and gave him a ball of thread.

7 Theseus tied the thread to <u>the window of the labyrinth</u>.

8 When Theseus found the Minotaur, <u>he ate it</u>.

9 Then <u>he followed Ariadne</u> back to the gate of the labyrinth.

5 The Wonderful Wings

Complete the puzzle. The name of the clever artist will appear in the centre of the puzzle. The first one has been done for you.

There was a clever artist who lived in (1). He had a nephew called (2), and a little son called (3).

The artist tried to kill his nephew, but Minerva, who was a (4), turned the young man into a bird.

The artist ran away to Crete. He made the King of Crete angry, and the King put him in (5).

The artist made some wonderful wings. He thought that he and his young son would escape by flying away to (6).

The wings worked well, but the boy flew too close to the (7). The heat melted the (8) on his wings, and the feathers came off. He fell into the sea and died.

6 Pluto and Persephone

Put the letters of these words in the right order. The first one has been done for you.

Pluto ruled the kingdom of the dead. He was very
(1) **onleyl** [lonely]. He did not have anyone to be his (2) **neqeu** [queen].

Pluto heard Persephone (3) **gninigs** [singing]. He went up towards the (4) **rEhta** [Earth] in his chariot. He caught (5) **hnporesPee** [Persephone] and took her to the kingdom of the dead.

Ceres did not know where her (6) **gahudert** [daughter] was. She was so sad that she forgot her duties, and the (7) **socrp** [crops] stopped growing.

(8) **tuloP** [Pluto] gave Persephone an apple. She ate (9) **flha** [half] of it. Jupiter said Persephone must stay with Pluto for half the year. She could stay with her (10) **hoterm** [mother] for the other half of the year.

7 A Wonderful Musician

Circle the right words or phrases to say what happened.

Eurydice died because (1) **an insect/a snake** bit her. Her (2) **husband/father**, Orpheus, decided to go to the kingdom of the dead to look for her.

Pluto agreed to let Eurydice go back with Orpheus, but he said Orpheus must not (3) **sing to her/look back at her** until he had left the kingdom of the dead. Orpheus (4) **obeyed/disobeyed** Pluto, and Eurydice had to stay behind.

Later some women tried to make Orpheus play (5) **happy/sad** music. He would not do as they asked and they (6) **laughed at/killed** him. Then Orpheus and Eurydice (7) **were together/never saw each other** again.

8 The Golden Chariot of the Sun

Put these sentences in the right order.

1 Phaeton wanted to know who his father was. ☐
2 He asked his mother to tell him where his father lived. ☐
3 Phaeton's friends did not believe that his father was Apollo. ☐
4 His mother told him that his father was Apollo, the sun-god. ☐
5 After a very long journey he reached Apollo's palace. ☐
6 Phaeton decided to go to India to ask his father to help him. ☐
7 She said that Apollo lived very far away, in India. ☐
8 He told his best friend: soon everyone knew about Phaeton's father. ☐
9 Phaeton wanted to show them that he was telling the truth. ☐

BOOK REPORT

Now write a book report to display in the library or your classroom. These questions will help you.

Title

Type What type of story is your book?

- Adventure
- Classic
- Crime
- Detective story
- Fairy tale
- Horror and suspense
- Mystery
- Play
- Romance
- Science fiction and fantasy
- Short story
- Others

Characters — Who are the main characters in the book?

Main characters — Describe the main characters. What do they look like? What are they like?

Story — What is the story about? Remember not to give the ending away!

My comments — What did you think of the story? Did you enjoy it? Would you recommend this book to your classmates?

Visit the website and download the book report template
www.oupchina.com.hk/elt/oper

OXFORD PROGRESSIVE ENGLISH READERS

Starter

The Ant and the Grasshopper and Other Stories by Aesop
Retold by David Foulds

The Brave Little Tailor and Other Stories by the Brothers Grimm
Retold by Katherine Mattock

The Emperor's New Clothes and Other Stories by Hans Christian Andersen
Retold by Janice Tibbetts

Folk Tales from Around the World
Retold by Rosemary Border

Giants, Dragons and Other Magical Creatures
Retold by Philip Popescu

Heroes and Heroines
Retold by Philip Popescu

In the Land of the Gods
Retold by Magnus Norberg

Journey to the West
Retold by Rosemary Border

The Lion and the Mouse and Other Stories by Aesop
Retold by David Foulds

The Little Mermaid and Other Stories by Hans Christian Andersen
Retold by Janice Tibbetts

The Monkey King
Retold by Rosemary Border

Peter Pan
Retold by Katherine Mattock

Level 1

Alice's Adventures in Wonderland
Lewis Carroll

The Call of the Wild and Other Stories
Jack London

Emma
Jane Austen

The Golden Goose and Other Stories
Retold by David Foulds

Jane Eyre
Charlotte Brontë

Just So Stories
Rudyard Kipling

Little Women
Louisa M. Alcott

The Lost Umbrella of Kim Chu
Eleanor Estes

The Secret Garden
Frances Hodgson Burnett

Tales from the Arabian Nights
Edited by David Foulds

Treasure Island
Robert Louis Stevenson

The Wizard of Oz
L. Frank Baum

Level 2

The Adventures of Sherlock Holmes
Sir Arthur Conan Doyle

A Christmas Carol
Charles Dickens

The Dagger with Wings and Other Father Brown Stories
G. K. Chesterton

The Flying Heads and Other Strange Stories
Edited by David Foulds

The Golden Touch and Other Stories
Edited by David Foulds

Gulliver's Travels — A Voyage to Lilliput
Jonathan Swift

The Jungle Book
Rudyard Kipling

Life Without Katy and Other Stories
O. Henry

Lord Jim
Joseph Conrad

A Midsummer Night's Dream and Other Stories from Shakespeare's Plays
Edited by David Foulds

The Mill on the Floss
George Eliot

Nicholas Nickleby
Charles Dickens

Oliver Twist
Charles Dickens

The Prince and the Pauper
Mark Twain

The Stone Junk and Other Stories
D. H. Howe

Stories from Greek Tragedies
Retold by Kieran McGovern

Stories from Shakespeare's Comedies
Retold by Katherine Mattock

Tales of King Arthur
Retold by David Foulds

The Talking Tree and Other Stories
David McRobbie

Through the Looking Glass
Lewis Carroll

Level 3

The Adventures of Huckleberry Finn
Mark Twain

The Adventures of Tom Sawyer
Mark Twain

Around the World in Eighty Days
Jules Verne

The Canterville Ghost and Other Stories
Oscar Wilde

David Copperfield
Charles Dickens

Fog and Other Stories
Bill Lowe

Further Adventures of Sherlock Holmes
Sir Arthur Conan Doyle

Great Expectations
Charles Dickens

Gulliver's Travels — Further Voyages
Jonathan Swift

The Hound of the Baskervilles
Sir Arthur Conan Doyle

The Merchant of Venice and Other Stories from Shakespeare's Plays
Edited by David Foulds

The Missing Scientist
S. F. Stevens

The Pickwick Papers
Charles Dickens

The Red Badge of Courage
Stephen Crane

Robinson Crusoe
Daniel Defoe

Silas Marner
George Eliot

Stories from Shakespeare's Histories
Retold by Katherine Mattock

A Tale of Two Cities
Charles Dickens

Tales of Crime and Detection
Edited by David Foulds

Two Boxes of Gold and Other Stories
Charles Dickens

LEVEL 4

Dr Jekyll and Mr Hyde and Other Stories
Robert Louis Stevenson

Far from the Madding Crowd
Thomas Hardy

From Russia, With Love
Ian Fleming

The Gifts and Other Stories
O. Henry and Others

The Good Earth
Pearl S. Buck

The Great Gatsby
F. Scott Fitzgerald

Journey to the Centre of the Earth
Jules Verne

King Solomon's Mines
H. Rider Haggard

Mansfield Park
Jane Austen

The Moonstone
Wilkie Collins

A Night of Terror and Other Strange Tales
Guy de Maupassant

Othello and Other Stories from Shakespeare's Plays
Edited by David Foulds

The Picture of Dorian Gray
Oscar Wilde

Seven Stories
H. G. Wells

Tales of Mystery and Imagination
Edgar Allan Poe

Tess of the d'Urbervilles
Thomas Hardy

The Thirty-nine Steps
John Buchan

Twenty Thousand Leagues Under the Sea
Jules Verne

The War of the Worlds
H. G. Wells

The Woman in White
Wilkie Collins

You Only Live Twice
Ian Fleming

LEVEL 5

The Diamond as Big as the Ritz and Other Stories
F. Scott Fitzgerald

Dracula
Bram Stoker

Dragon Seed
Pearl S. Buck

Frankenstein
Mary Shelley

Kidnapped
Robert Louis Stevenson

Lorna Doone
R. D. Blackmore

The Mayor of Casterbridge
Thomas Hardy

The Old Wives' Tale
Arnold Bennett

Pride and Prejudice
Jane Austen

The Stalled Ox and Other Stories
Saki

Three Men in a Boat
Jerome K. Jerome

Vanity Fair
William Thackeray

Wuthering Heights
Emily Brontë